THE ULTIMATE
FOOTBALL
QUIZ BOOK

Quiz Kingdom

x

First Published 2022 by Paw Kingdom Limited

Text & illustrations © Spencer Miller & Harrison Florio

For printing information see the inside cover of this book.

www.PawKingdom.co.uk

CONTENTS!

Welcome to Quiz Kingdom!

Hey there! We are Quiz Kingdom and, as the name suggests, we love quizzes! Our quiz books are the perfect way to test your knowledge against friends and family and learn something along the way!

How it Works!

Every question has three options: A, B & C. If you need to make it harder, ask the reader not to give you the options! The bonus question on each round does not come with any options, and it is closest wins, so give it your best guess! Each round has five difficulty levels:

Easy

Medium

Hard

Expert

Master

BONUS QUESTION! **Impossible!**

If you enjoy please consider leaving a review and make sure to check out Quiz Kingdom's other books on Amazon.com!
Thank you!

CHAPTER 1:
English Football

1
Which team has finished runners-up in the Premier League twice without ever winning it?

A	Newcastle
B	Aston Villa
C	Tottenham Hotspur

2
Who scored the quickest goal in Premier League history in 2019?

A	Danny Ings
B	Charlie Austin
C	Shane Long

3
Which of these players won the most PFA Fans' Player of the Year award?

A	Steven Gerrard
B	Paul Scholes
C	Frank Lampard

4
Who is the highest scoring player in the Premier League that does not originate from England?

A	Thierry Henry
B	Robin Van Persie
C	Sergio Aguero

Answers on Page: 66

5 Which manager has won the most Premier League Manager of the Month awards in one season?

A Pep Guardiola

B Jurgen Klopp

C Sir Alex Ferguson

6 How many Welsh clubs have competed in the Premier League?

A 1

B 2

C 3

7 Which manager has had the longest spell in charge of a Premier League club?

A Arsene Wenger

B Sir Alex Ferguson

C Sean Dyche

8 Jamie Vardy broke the record for scoring in consecutive games. How many games in a row did he score in during the 2015/16 season?

A 9

B 10

C 11

Answers on Page: 66

9 Which teams participated in the Premier League's all-time highest scoring match of 7-4 in 2007?

A Blackburn & Manchester United

B Tottenham Hotspur & Wigan Athletic

C Portsmouth & Reading

10 How many teams will participate in the Premier League for the 2022/23 season, that originate from London?

A 6

B 7

C 8

11 Which manager has won the most consecutive Premier League Manager of the Month awards?

A Jurgen Klopp

B Pep Guardiola

C Jose Mourinho

12 Who scored the fastest hat-trick in Premier League history?

A Harry Kane

B Mohamed Salah

C Sadio Mane

Answers on Page: 66

13 Which of these players have not made 500 Premier League appearances for one club?

A | Jamie Carragher

B | Steven Gerrard

C | Paul Scholes

14 In what year was the Premier League founded?

A | 1990

B | 1992

C | 1994

15 Which team recorded the fewest amount of wins in a single Premier League season?

A | Coventry City

B | Derby County

C | Sunderland

16 How many clubs have played in the Premier League?

A | 46

B | 48

C | 50

Answers on Page: 66

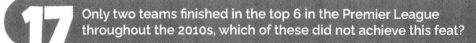

17 Only two teams finished in the top 6 in the Premier League throughout the 2010s, which of these did not achieve this feat?

A	Tottenham Hotspur
B	Liverpool
C	Manchester City

18 Who won, and subsequently converted, the 89th minute winning penalty in the 2021 Community Shield for Leicester City?

A	Kelechi Iheanacho
B	Jamie Vardy
C	Youri Tielemans

19 Which Premier League team became the first team to represent England in the inaugural European Conference League?

A	West Ham
B	Leicester City
C	Tottenham Hotspur

20 Which manager has managed the most clubs in the Premier League?

A	Sam Allardyce
B	Mark Hughes
C	Roy Hodgson

Answers on Page: 66

21

In the 2017/18 season, Manchester City won the league by a record margin ahead of 2nd place Manchester United. What was the points difference between the two clubs?

A 11

B 15

C 19

22

Who is the only player outside the United Kingdom to make over 500 Premier League appearances?

A Brad Friedel

B Petr Cech

C Mark Schwarzer

23

Which player has won the most Premier League Golden Boots, with four trophies?

A Harry Kane

B Thierry Henry

C Alan Shearer

24

Who scored the first hat-trick of the 2021/22 Premier League season on the opening day?

A Bruno Fernandes

B Son Heung-Min

C Mohamed Salah

25 Who scored the decisive penalty for Liverpool to win the 2022 FA Cup Final vs Chelsea?

A Sadio Mane

B Diogo Jota

C Kostas Tsimikas

Sergio Aguero broke who's Premier League record for most goals scored with one club at the end of the 2020/21 season?

A Alan Shearer

B Thierry Henry

C Wayne Rooney

27 Who is the youngest player in Premier League history to score in seven successive games?

A Bukayo Saka

B Joe Willock

C Phil Foden

In the 2018/19 season, Manchester City and Huddersfield broke the record for biggest margin between the champions and the bottom-placed club. How many points were between them?

A 79

B 82

C 88

29 Which of these teams have never been relegated from the Premier League?

A Brighton & Hove Albion

B Manchester City

C West Ham

30 Which team holds the record for the most yellow cards in one season in Premier League history, with 101 yellow cards?

A Arsenal

B Manchester City

C Leeds United

31 In the 2020/21 season, Fulham set a new record for the fewest goals scored at home in a season. How many goals did they score?

A 9

B 12

C 14

32 Arsenal were the first Premier League team to do what during the 2001/02 season?

A Go unbeaten all season

B Go unbeaten away all season

C Go unbeaten at home all season

33 Which club is the only team to finish in the top six with a negative goal difference?

A Manchester United

B Norwich

C Blackburn

Which club conceded the fewest home goals in a single Premier League season?

A Manchester United

B Chelsea

C Liverpool

35 In the 2021/22 season, which team became the first in Premier League history to have gone through a whole season without being behind at half-time?

A Manchester City

B Chelsea

C Liverpool

Which team was relegated in the 1996/97 season because they were deducted three points for failing to play a fixture?

A Sunderland

B Nottingham Forest

C Middlesbrough

Answers on Page: 67

37

Who is the only player to win the PFA Footballer of the Year award whilst playing for a team that finished in the bottom half of the table?

A Paul McGrath

B David Ginola

C Kevin Phillips

38

Which team holds the record for 20 consecutive losses in the Premier League?

A Sunderland

B Derby County

C Huddersfield

39

Which club holds the record for the lowest points tally for a club that has stayed up, with just 34 points?

A Norwich City

B Portsmouth

C West Brom

40

Liverpool scored a record number of away goals during the 2013/14 season. How many goals did they score in their 19 away games?

A 41

B 45

C 48

Answers on Page: 67

BONUS QUESTION!

How many hat-tricks were there in the 1993/94 season?

Answers on Page: 67

CHAPTER 2: European Cups

1 How many teams represented England in the 2021/22 Europa League?

A 2

B 3

C 4

2 Who received the Man of the Match award in the 2021 European Super Cup?

A Kepa Arrizabalaga

B Gerard Moreno

C Kai Havertz

3 What rule was abolished for European competitions in the 2021/22 season?

A Two legs for knockout games

B Five substitutions allowed during normal time

C The Away Goals rule

4 Which club made their competition debut in 2021/22 Europa League?

A West Ham

B Leicester City

C Lazio

Answers on Page: 68

5 Real Madrid won the 2021/22 Champions League. How many times have they now won the competition?

A 13

B 14

C 15

6 The amount of teams in the Europa League group stage was reduced from 48 to how many teams for the 2021/22 season?

A 24

B 28

C 32

7 Which team has won the most Europa League titles in the history of the competition?

A Sevilla

B Atletico Madrid

C Liverpool

8 Which coach has won the most finals in Champions League history?

A Carlo Ancelotti

B Zinedine Zidane

C Bob Paisley

Answers on Page: 68

9 Who won the first ever Champions League in 1955?

A	Barcelona
B	Real Madrid
C	AC Milan

10 How many teams represented Spain in the 2021/22 Champions League?

A	3
B	4
C	5

11 Who is the English top goal scorer in Champions League history?

A	Steven Gerrard
B	Wayne Rooney
C	Frank Lampard

12 Which club made their competition debut in 2021/22 Champions League?

A	Sheriff
B	Young Boys
C	Malmo

Answers on Page: 68

13
In the Champions League era, which player has scored the most goals in the Champions League Final?

A Lionel Messi

B Samuel Eto'o

C Cristiano Ronaldo

14
Which striker has the most red cards in the Champions League, with four?

A Wayne Rooney

B Zlatan Ibrahimovic

C Didier Drogba

15
Who won the UEFA Champions League final in 2004?

A AC Milan

B AS Monaco

C FC Porto

16
Which player holds the record for the most amount of assists in Champions League history?

A Cristiano Ronaldo

B Lionel Messi

C Ryan Giggs

Answers on Page: 68

17 Who scored the winning goal in the 1999 Champions League Final between Bayern Munich and Manchester United?

A Teddy Sheringham

B Ole Gunnar Solskjaer

C David Beckham

18 Who is the only player to win the Champions League with three different clubs?

A Samuel Eto'o

B Mateo Kovacic

C Clarence Seedorf

19 Who won UEFA Champions League Final in 2001?

A Bayern Munich

B Real Madrid

C Valencia

20 Who was the first Portuguese team to win the Europa League?

A Benfica

B FC Porto

C Sporting Lisbon

Answers on Page: 68

21 Which team was the first British team to lift the European Cup?

A Liverpool

B Manchester United

C Celtic

Which Dutch club achieved three consecutive European Cup wins from 1971 to 1973?

A PSV

B Ajax

C Feyenoord

23 Who became the first defender to score in two Champions League Finals?

A Sergio Ramos

B Diego Godin

C Paolo Maldini

Which club was the second club to win the Champions League?

A Benfica

B Frankfurt

C Inter Milan

nswers on Page: 68

25 Which stadium won the rights to hold the 2003 Champions League Final for the first time?

A Amsterdam Arena

B Luzhniki Stadium

C Old Trafford

Which Champions League Final was the first-ever to have an extra time? 26

A Celtic v Inter Milan *(1967)*

B Real Madrid vs AC Milan *(1958)*

C Barcelona vs Benfica *(1961)*

27 Who were the first team to win the Champions League the year after winning the Europa League?

A FC Porto

B Chelsea

C Liverpool

Who were the first team to have won the Champions League without being champions of their domestic league? 28

A Inter Milan

B Bayern Munich

C Nottingham Forest

Answers on Page: 69

29 Who was the first player sent off in a Champions League final?

A Juan Cuadrado

B Didier Drogba

C Jens Lehmann

30 Which Liverpool goalkeeper first performed his famous 'Spaghetti Legs' antics in the Champions League?

A Pepe Reina

B Bruce Grobbelaar

C Jerzy Dudek

31 Who scored the opening goal in the 1999 Champions League Final between Manchester United and Bayern Munich?

A Mario Basler

B Stefan Effenberg

C Lothar Matthaus

32 Who was the first Englishman to score in a Champions League Final for a foreign club?

A David Beckham

B Steven McManaman

C Gary Lineker

33 Who was the first captain to score in a Champions League Final?

A Stefan Effenberg

B Steven Gerrard

C Raul Gonzalez

Who scored the only goal in the 1978 European Cup Final between Liverpool and Club Brugge? 34

A Terry McDermott

B Alan Kennedy

C Kenny Dalglish

35 The first penalty shootout to decide the Champions League happened in which final?

A Liverpool vs Roma

B Steaua Bucuresti vs Barcelona

C PSV vs Benfica

Which city hosted the first ever UEFA Champions League Final? 36

A London

B Paris

C Rome

Answers on Page: 69

37 Which of these teams did Nottingham Forest not defeat in a Champions League Final?

A Malmo

B Hamburg

C Club Brugge

Which player holds the record number of assists in a Champions League season from a Premier League club? 38

A James Milner

B Wayne Rooney

C Roberto Firmino

39 The first Champions League Final to go to a replay was during which season?

A 1971/72

B 1973/74

C 1975/76

Who scored 4 goals in the 1960 European Cup Final? 40

A Ferenc Puskas

B Luis del Sol

C Alfredo Di Stefano

BONUS QUESTION!

How many Champions League appearances did Barcelona legend Xavi make?

Answers on Page: 69

CHAPTER 3:
International Football

1
Who was England's captain when they won the World Cup in 1966?

A	Bobby Moore
B	Bobby Charlton
C	Gordon Banks

2
How many World Cups have France won?

A	1
B	2
C	3

3
Which of the following teams have won the Copa America the fewest times?

A	Argentina
B	Brazil
C	Uruguay

4
Which of the following players achieved the fewest international caps?

A	Sergio Ramos
B	Gianluigi Buffon
C	Iker Casillas

Answers on Page: 70

5 Who won the first ever World Cup?

A Uruguay

B Italy

C Brazil

6 Which nation won the 2004 Euro Championships?

A Denmark

B Greece

C France

7 Which of these teams have never won the World Cup in back-to-back tournaments?

A Italy

B Brazil

C Germany

8 Who won Young Player of the Tournament at Euro 2020?

A Chiesa

B Pedri

C Rice

Answers on Page: 70

9
Which team have won the African Cup of Nations the most times?

A Egypt

B South Africa

C Tunisia

10
How many different World Cup winners have there been?

A 6

B 8

C 10

11
For Euro 2020, the Spanish national team failed to call up any players from which of these clubs?

A Barcelona

B Real Madrid

C Atletico Madrid

12
What is the only team to have reached the last 16 of every World Cup?

A Germany

B Italy

C Brazil

Answers on Page: 70

13 What is the nickname of Nigeria's national team?

A The Super Eagles

B The Flying Nigerians

C The Super Falcons

Which nation is the only nation to win two consecutive Euro titles? **14**

A Soviet Union

B Germany

C Spain

15 What is the only nation to appear at every World Cup finals?

A Uruguay

B Brazil

C France

Which player is the all-time top scorer in the African Cup of Nations? **16**

A Didier Drogba

B Samuel Eto'o

C Laurent Pokou

Answers on Page: 70

17 Which team has made the most Copa America Final appearances?

A	Argentina
B	Brazil
C	Chile

18 How many teams will be included in the 2026 World Cup?

A	32
B	38
C	48

19 Who were the latest team to go unbeaten at a World Cup but did not end up as champions?

A	Cameroon
B	Belgium
C	New Zealand

20 Which nation was the first host nation to be eliminated in the first round of the World Cup finals?

A	South Africa
B	Sweden
C	Japan

Answers on Page: 70

21
Which of these World Cup winning nations have also never lost in the final of the World Cup?

A | Brazil

B | Uruguay

C | Italy

22
The 2021 Copa America was supposed to be hosted for the first time in more than one country but did not due to the COVID-19 Pandemic, which countries were supposed to be the hosts?

A | Argentina and Colombia

B | Brazil and Uruguay

C | Peru and Chile

23
Which of these teams were absent for the World Cup in 1930?

A | United States

B | France

C | England

24
As of Summer 2022, how many different countries have hosted the World Cup during the 21 tournaments that have taken place?

A | 15

B | 17

C | 19

Answers on Page: 70

25 Which continent boycotted the 1966 World Cup?

A	Africa
B	Asia
C	North America

26 What is the only nation to win both the mens and womens World Cup?

A	Spain
B	Brazil
C	Germany

27 From 1960 until 1976, how many teams competed in the Euro Championships?

A	4
B	12
C	24

28 What is the oldest international football competition contested between men's national teams?

A	World Cup
B	Copa America
C	AFCON

Answers on Page: 71

29
Germany won the 1996 Euro Final on Golden Goal for the first time against which nation?

A Denmark

B Italy

C Czech Republic

30
The 1968 Euro Championship Semi-Final between Italy and the Soviet Union was decided by what?

A Penalty Shootout

B Coin Toss

C Golden Goal

31
Which country has lost the World Cup Final the most times?

A Netherlands

B Argentina

C Germany

32
Euro 2000 was the first tournament to be hosted by two countries, what were the nations?

A Belgium and Netherlands

B Austria and Switzerland

C Poland and Ukraine

33

In the 2001 Copa America, which team set a record by not just going undefeated, but also did not concede a single goal as they won every single match during the competition?

A Chile

B Colombia

C Uruguay

34

What country was the first to wear names on the back of their shirts at World Cup Finals?

A England

B Brazil

C Germany

35

Which player has played the most minutes at the World Cup Finals?

A Paolo Maldini

B Miroslav Klose

C Diego Maradona

36

The 2016 Copa America was held outside of South America for the first time, where was it hosted?

A Spain

B Mexico

C USA

Answers on Page: 71

37
Who is the only player to play in three World Cup Finals?

A Pele

B Cafu

C Garrincha

38
When was the first AFCON tournament, with Egypt, Sudan and Ethiopia being the only participating teams?

A 1951

B 1957

C 1963

39
Out of all the World Cup winners, which club has provided the most?

A Inter Milan

B Juventus

C AS Roma

40
How many penalties were taken during the shoot-out in the 2015 AFCON Final between Ivory Coast and Ghana?

A 6

B 14

C 22

nswers on Page: 71

BONUS QUESTION!

How many minutes were 2018 World Cup winners France behind their opponents throughout the tournament?

Answers on Page: 71

CHAPTER 4:
European Leagues

1 Who won the 2021/22 Bundesliga title?

A RB Leipzig

B Borussia Dortmund

C Bayern Munich

2 Which team has the most La Liga titles?

A Barcelona

B Real Madrid

C Atletico Madrid

3 Who won the 2020/21 Ligue 1 title?

A PSG

B Lyon

C Lille

4 Who is the only African footballer to win the La Liga Golden Boot?

A Samuel Eto'o

B Pierre-Emerick Aubameyang

C Emmanuel Adebayor

Answers on Page: 72

5 Which Serie A team was relegated in 2006 due to the Calciopoli Match Fixing Scandal?

A Lazio

B Fiorentina

C Juventus

Which Italian club did Diego Maradona play for? **6**

A Juventus

B Napoli

C Inter Milan

7 Who did Kylian Mbappe overtake as Monaco's youngest ever goalscorer?

A Thierry Henry

B David Trezeguet

C Thomas Lemar

What is the nickname for the Italian club Inter Milan? **8**

A Nerazzurri

B Rossoneri

C Bianconeri

Answers on Page: 72

9 Which is the only club, other than Real Madrid and Barcelona, never to have played outside the Spanish top division?

A Atletico Madrid

B Valencia

C Athletic Bilbao

10 Paul Gascoigne played in the Serie A between 1992 and 1995 but for which team?

A Roma

B Lazio

C Napoli

11 Which club in Spain has finished runners-up in the La Liga the most number of times?

A Real Madrid

B Barcelona

C Atletico Madrid

12 AC Milan and Inter Milan's stadium, the San Siro, is also known as what?

A Stadio Giuseppe Meazza

B Stadio Delle Alpi

C Stadio Ferraris

Answers on Page: 72

13 Which Ligue 1 side holds the record for most consecutive titles?

A PSG

B Saint-Etienne

C Lyon

14 Which two Italian teams have won 19 titles and been runners-up 16 times each as of the end of the 2021/22 season?

A AC Milan and Inter Milan

B Roma and AC Milan

C Genoa and Inter Milan

15 Which Bundesliga club did Kevin Keegan play for in the 1970s?

A Borussia Monchengladbach

B Hamburger SV

C Schalke

16 Which Italian club went unbeaten the entire 1991/92 season?

A AC Milan

B Juventus

C Inter Milan

Answers on Page: 72

17 Which club won the La Liga title in successive years in 1983 and 1984?

A	Athletic Bilbao
B	Valencia
C	Barcelona

18 In 2015, how many minutes did it take Robert Lewandowski to score five goals for Bayern Munich against Wolfsburg?

A	7
B	9
C	11

19 Which player holds the record for most Ligue 1 titles with 8 championships?

A	Juninho Pernambucano
B	Thiago Silva
C	Marco Verratti

20 Who won the 2000/01 Serie A season?

A	Lazio
B	Roma
C	Juventus

Answers on Page: 72

21 What did Alessandro Del Piero do on his first start for Juventus?

A Score a hat-trick

B Get sent off

C Miss a penalty

Who won the 1999/2000 La Liga? 22

A Sevilla

B Deportivo La Coruna

C Real Sociedad

23 Who holds the record for most goals scored in the Bundesliga?

A Gerd Muller

B Robert Lewandowski

C Claudio Pizarro

Who are the Bundesliga's second most successful team? 24

A Nuremberg

B Schalke

C Borussia Dortmund

nswers on Page: 72

25 How many teams have won the La Liga?

A 5

B 7

C 9

26 Who among these players has won the league with both Barcelona and Real Madrid?

A Luis Figo

B Albert Celades

C Ronaldo

27 AC Milan won the title in 1994, but how many goals did they score in the 34 league games?

A 36

B 58

C 80

28 Which manager took Mainz to their highest ever league finish?

A Bo Svensson

B Jurgen Klopp

C Thomas Tuchel

Answers on Page: 73

29 Which team in the Bundesliga was the only ever-present team in the league until their relegation in 2018?

A Wolfsburg

B Hamburger SV

C Koln

30 Which of these teams have not gone undefeated in the entire history of the La Liga?

A Barcelona

B Real Madrid

C Athletic Bilbao

31 Who is the record top goalscorer in Serie A history?

A Antonio Di Natale

B Francesco Totti

C Silvio Piola

32 What year was the Bundesliga founded?

A 1959

B 1963

C 1966

33 Which Ligue 1 side holds the record for fewest losses in a single season?

A Nantes

B PSG

C Marseille

AC Milan hold the Serie A record for the longest unbeaten streak, how many games did they go unbeaten? **34**

A 50

B 54

C 58

35 PSG have the record for the most points in a single Ligue 1 season, how many points did they achieve?

A 93

B 96

C 99

In what year was the La Liga formed? **36**

A 1925

B 1929

C 1934

Answers on Page: 73

37 Valenciennes suffered the biggest defeat in Ligue 1 history when they lost 12-1, but to which team did they lose?

A PSG

B Saint-Etienne

C Sochaux

In what year was Ligue 1 founded? **38**

A 1929

B 1932

C 1935

39 The founders of AC Milan came from which English city?

A Nottingham

B Sheffield

C Leicester

Serie A is the oldest current top flight league in Europe's top 5 leagues, but when was it founded? **40**

A 1896

B 1898

C 1900

Answers on Page: 73

BONUS QUESTION!

How many goals and assists did Lionel Messi end his final La Liga season with in 2021?

Answers on Page: 73

CHAPTER 5:

Transfers

1 Which manager was renowned for speaking to the media on transfer deadline day through his car window?

A Harry Redknapp

B Steve Bruce

C Roy Hodgson

2 Who was the first ever galactico to be purchased by Real Madrid president Florentino Perez in 2000?

A Steve Mcmanaman

B Luis Figo

C David Beckham

3 Which player famously drove themselves to QPR on deadline day to complete a transfer which fell through before the deadline?

A Peter Odemwingie

B Benjani

C Saido Berahino

4 Which Champions League winner joined Leicester City in 2014?

A Sulley Muntari

B Dejan Stankovic

C Esteban Cambiasso

Answers on Page: 74

5 Which player features three times in footballs 50 most expensive transfers list?

A Romelu Lukaku

B Cristiano Ronaldo

C Angel Di Maria

6 Carlos Tevez and which other Argentine completed shock moves to West Ham in 2006?

A Gabriel Heinze

B Maxi Rodriguez

C Javier Mascherano

7 Who holds the record for the highest transfer fee paid for a manager?

A Julian Nagelsmann

B Jose Mourinho

C Andre-Villas Boas

8 Who is the most expensive signing in Premier League history?

A Paul Pogba

B Jack Grealish

C Romelu Lukaku

Answers on Page: 74

Transfers

9 Qatar Sports Investments took over PSG in 2011. Who was the club's most expensive signing in their first transfer window as owners?

A Zlatan Ibrahimovic

B Javier Pastore

C Thiago Silva

10 Which club was Ronaldinho's first European club?

A Barcelona

B AC Milan

C PSG

11 Who is the most expensive signing in La Liga history?

A Philippe Coutinho

B Joao Felix

C Antoine Griezmann

12 Who is the most expensive British manager of all-time?

A Frank Lampard

B Mark Hughes

C Brendan Rodgers

Answers on Page: 74

13 Where did Real Madrid sign Casemiro from?

A Santos

B São Paulo

C Corinthians

14 Who did Liverpool replace Fernando Torres with on the same day he left for Chelsea in 2011?

A Luis Suarez

B Craig Bellamy

C Andy Carroll

15 How many times has Jose Mourinho signed Nemanja Matic?

A 1

B 2

C 3

16 Who was Pep Guardiola's first signing at Manchester City?

A Oleksandr Zinchenko

B Ilkay Gundogan

C Nolito

17 Who is the most expensive signing in Bundesliga history?

A Lucas Hernandez

B Leroy Sane

C Dayot Upamecano

18 Which of these Chelsea youth graduates left the club in 2021 for the most amount of money?

A Marc Guehi

B Tammy Abraham

C Fikayo Tomori

19 Which player holds the record for highest transfer fee for an African player?

A Pierre-Emerick Aubameyang

B Nicolas Pepe

C Riyad Mahrez

20 Who did Edwin Van der Sar join Manchester United from?

A Ajax

B Juventus

C Fulham

Answers on Page: 74

21
Which player holds the Chinese Super League record for highest transfer fee with a £52 million move?

A Oscar

B Hulk

C Paulinho

22
Who is the most expensive South American Striker of all time as of July 2022?

A Gonzalo Higuain

B Luis Suarez

C Darwin Nunez

23
When Cristian Vieri left Lazio for Inter Milan in 1999 for a world-record £32.5million, who did Lazio then break the record for as a replacement in a £35million deal?

A Hernan Crespo

B Claudio Lopez

C Marcelo Salas

24
Which team spent the most money in the 2021 summer transfer window?

A Manchester United

B Arsenal

C Manchester City

nswers on Page: 74

25 Who joined Juventus from Fiorentina for a then world-record fee of £8million in 1990?

A Roberto Baggio

B Gianluca Vialli

C Gianluigi Lentini

26 Real Madrid broke the transfer record fee five times in a row between 2000-2013, which of these players did not break a record fee?

A Zinedine Zidane

B Ronaldo

C Luis Figo

27 Who was the first player Mikel Arteta brought into Arsenal as manager?

A Cedric Soares

B Willian

C Pablo Mari

28 What non-Premier League team spent the most money in the 2021 Summer Transfer Window?

A PSG

B Atletico Madrid

C Roma

Answers on Page: 75

29 Who was the only player Manchester United officially signed in January 2021?

A Facundo Pellistri

B Bruno Fernandes

C Amad Diallo

30 Which of these teams did not break the world-record transfer fee for Ronaldo?

A Barcelona

B PSV

C Inter Milan

31 Who was Jurgen Klopp's first signing at Liverpool?

A Marko Grujic

B Steven Caulker

C Sadio Mane

32 Newcastle broke the world-record transfer fee when they signed Alan Shearer from Blackburn in 1996, but how much did he go for?

A £13million

B £15million

C £19million

Answers on Page: 75

33 Who is Napoli's all-time record transfer signing?

A Gonzalo Higuain

B Hirving Lozano

C Victor Osimhen

34 Who broke the transfer record in 1987 after Diego Maradona had broken the record two times in a row?

A Ruud Gullit

B Roberto Baggio

C Paolo Rossi

35 Which of these strikers were signed by Chelsea on a permanent deal?

A Alexandre Pato

B Falcao

C Samuel Eto'o

36 Who is Real Madrid's record transfer signing for a midfielder?

A Aurelien Tchouameni

B Kaka

C James Rodriguez

Answers on Page: 75

37
What is the only European club that Brazilian legend Socrates played for?

A Valencia

B Fiorentina

C PSG

38
What Italian manager made his debut in the Premier League for Leicester City aged 36?

A Marcello Lippi

B Antonio Conte

C Roberto Mancini

39
Who did AC Milan sign for a then record fee of £10million in 1992?

A Gianluigi Lentini

B Jean-Pierre Papin

C Brian Laudrup

40
Who was the first ever 1 million pound player?

A Giuseppe Savoldi

B Trevor Francis

C Gary Lineker

BONUS QUESTION!

What is the reported total cumulative transfer fees that has been spent on Romelu Lukaku?

Answers on Page: 75

ANSWERS!

1. A - Newcastle
2. C - Shane Long
3. A - Steven Gerrard
4. C - Sergio Aguero
5. B - Jurgen Klopp
6. B - 2
7. A - Arsene Wenger
8. C - 11

9. C - Portsmouth & Reading
10. B - 7
11. B - Pep Guardiola
12. C - Sadio Mane
13. C - Paul Scholes
14. B - 1992
15. B - Derby County
16. C - 50

17. B - Liverpool
18. A - Kelechi Iheanacho
19. C - Tottenham Hotspur
20. A - Sam Allardyce
21. C - 19
22. C - Mark Schwarzer
23. B - Thierry Henry
24. A - Bruno Fernandes

25. C - Kostas Tsimikas

26. C - Wayne Rooney

27. B - Joe Willock

28. B - 82

29. A - Brighton & Hove Albion

30. C - Leeds United

31. A - 9

32. B - Go unbeaten away all season

33. B - Norwich

34. A - Manchester United

35. B - Chelsea

36. C - Middlesbrough

37. B - David Ginola

38. A - Sunderland

39. C - West Brom

40. C - 48

BONUS QUESTION!

19 hat-tricks

1. A - 2
2. B - Gerard Moreno
3. C - Away Goals rule
4. A - West Ham
5. B - 14
6. C - 32
7. A - Sevilla
8. A - Carlo Ancelotti

9. B - Real Madrid
10. C - 5
11. B - Wayne Rooney
12. A - Sheriff
13. C - Cristiano Ronaldo
14. B - Zlatan Ibrahimovic
15. C - FC Porto
16. A - Cristiano Ronaldo

17. B - Ole Gunnar Solskjær
18. C - Clarence Seedorf
19. A - Bayern Munich
20. B - FC Porto
21. C - Celtic
22. B - Ajax
23. A - Sergio Ramos
24. A - Benfica

25. C - Old Trafford

26. B - Real Madrid vs AC Milan (1958)

27. A - FC Porto

28. C - Nottingham Forest

29. C - Jens Lehmann

30. B - Bruce Grobbelaar

31. A - Mario Basler

32. B - Steven McManaman

33. A - Stefan Effenberg

34. C - Kenny Dalglish

35. A - Liverpool vs Roma

36. B - Paris

37. C - Club Brugge

38. A - James Milner

39. B - 1973/74

40. A - Ferenc Puskas

BONUS QUESTION!

151

1. A - Bobby Moore
2. B - 2
3. B - Brazil
4. C - Iker Casillas
5. A - Uruguay
6. B - Greece
7. C - Germany
8. B - Pedri

9. A - Egypt
10. B - 8
11. B - Real Madrid
12. C - Brazil
13. A - The Super Eagles
14. C - Spain
15. B - Brazil
16. B - Samuel Eto'o

17. A - Argentina
18. C - 48
19. C - New Zealand
20. A - South Africa
21. B - Uruguay
22. A - Argentina and Colombia
23. C - England
24. B - 17

25. A - Africa

26. C - Germany

27. A - 4

28. B - Copa America

29. C - Czech Republic

30. B - Coin Toss

31. C - Germany

32. A - Belgium and Netherlands

33. B - Colombia

34. A - England

35. A - Paolo Maldini

36. C - USA

37. B - Cafu

38. B - 1957

39. B - Juventus

40. C - 22

BONUS QUESTION!

9 minutes

1. C - Bayern Munich
2. B - Real Madrid
3. C - Lille
4. A - Samuel Eto'o
5. C - Juventus
6. B - Napoli
7. A - Thierry Henry
8. A - Nerazzurri

9. C - Athletic Bilbao
10. B - Lazio
11. B - Barcelona
12. A - Stadio Giuseppe Meazza
13. C - Lyon
14. A - AC Milan and Inter Milan
15. B - Hamburger SV
16. A - AC Milan

17. A - Athletic Bilbao
18. B - 9
19. C - Marco Verratti
20. B - Roma
21. A - Score a hat-trick
22. B - Deportivo La Coruna
23. A - Gerd Muller
24. A - Nuremberg

25. C - 9

26. B - Albert Celades

27. A - 36

28. C - Thomas Tuchel

29. B - Hamburger SV

30. A - Barcelona

31. C - Silvio Piola

32. B - 1963

33. A - Nantes

34. C - 58

35. B - 96

36. B - 1929

37. C - Sochaux

38. B - 1932

39. A - Nottingham

40. B - 1898

BONUS QUESTION!

30 goals and 9 assists

1. A - Harry Redknapp
2. B - Luis Figo
3. A - Peter Odemwingie
4. C - Esteban Cambiasso
5. A - Romelu Lukaku
6. C - Javier Mascherano
7. A - Julian Nagelsmann
8. B - Jack Grealish

9. B - Javier Pastore
10. C - PSG
11. A - Philippe Coutinho
12. C - Brendan Rodgers
13. B - São Paulo
14. C - Andy Carroll
15. C - 3
16. B - Ilkay Gundogan

17. A - Lucas Hernandez
18. B - Tammy Abraham
19. B - Nicolas Pepe
20. C - Fulham
21. A - Oscar
22. A - Gonzalo Higuain
23. A - Hernan Crespo
24. B - Arsenal

25. A - Roberto Baggio

26. B - Ronaldo

27. C - Pablo Mari

28. C - Roma

29. C - Amad Diallo

30. B - PSV

31. A - Marko Grujic

32. B - £15million

33. C - Victor Osimhen

34. A - Ruud Gullit

35. C - Samuel Eto'o

36. A - Aurelien Tchouameni

37. B - Fiorentina

38. C - Roberto Mancini

39. B - Jean-Pierre Papin

40. A - Giuseppe Savoldi

BONUS QUESTION!

£293.5 million

Printed in Great Britain
by Amazon